WHOSAURUS? DINOSAURUS!

EEK!

WHOSAURUS?
DINOSAURUS!
ALISON PRINCE
JANE HICKSON

Studio Vista a division of
Cassell & Collier Macmillan Publishers Limited
35 Red Lion Square, London WC1R 4SG
Sydney, Auckland, Toronto, Johannesburg

An affiliate of Macmillan Inc., New York

Printed in Great Britain

ISBN 0 289 70556 8

Are you a little vague about dinosaurs?

No wonder. In spite of the long names and the skeletons in the museums, there's an awful lot we don't know about them. Dinosaurs are, in fact,

A GREAT UNSOLVED MYSTERY.

They disappeared quite suddenly and all at once, about sixty-five million years ago, and we don't know why.

Just think how long it is from the time when the first primitive man appeared until now – the moment when you are reading this. Give or take a few hundred centuries, it's about three million years.

But when the first hairy men evolved, there were no dinosaurs left, and had been none for *sixty-two million years*. No dinosaurs. There were lizards and frogs and birds and lots of furry little mammals which would, in time, become dogs and cats and cows and all the beasts which you see in the zoo – but no dinosaurs.

We don't think dinosaurs ever got round to doing much in the technical field because they had very small brains.

So they probably didn't take off to another planet in a fleet of space ships. What *did* happen to them?

Did the dinosaur ladies decide to stop laying eggs? A prehistoric Women's Lib. movement seems unlikely, but you never know.

Maybe the weather turned cold and they never got round to dressmaking.

Maybe the meat-eating dinosaurs ate all the plant-eating dinosaurs and then died of starvation. Maybe they were too successful and ended up without any elbow-room, just as we may do if we're not careful.

Or perhaps they just bored each other to death.

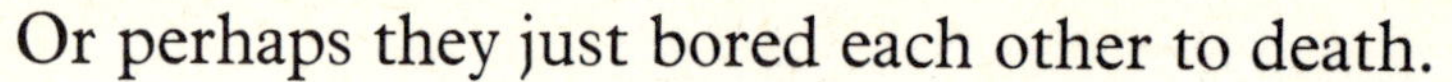

Whatever it was, the disappearance of the dinosaurs remains

A GREAT UNSOLVED MYSTERY

It would be a fascinating mystery to solve, since it might shed some light on our own future. The dinosaurs lived far, far longer than we have done so far, and if we knew why they failed, it might give us a clue about what lies in store for us.

So, like any detective worth his do-it-yourself fingerprint kit, we will examine the case history.

Dinosaurs lived way back, when the world was as warm and soft as a new loaf. The sea covered most of the earth and what dry land there was must have been a steamy, sploshy place to live in.

With all this water about, some funny things happened. When the earth began to dry out, chalk from the water was left behind, rather as scale is left in a kettle. It was this chalk which made the white cliffs of Dover. And – here's a thought – by the time those cliffs had formed, the last dinosaurs had died out.

FOR MILLIONS OF YEARS THE WORLD WAS SMOOTH ....
NICE FOR DINOSAURS
NOT SO NICE
NASTY FOR DINOSAURS
DINOSAURS GONE
WHAT WILL HAPPEN TO IT NEXT?

The dinosaurs seem to have given up the ghost when the world gave up its water. The earth must have been a smooth, moist place when it was new, rather like a ripe plum. When a plum dries it shrivels. The skin of a prune is all ridges and hollows and perhaps in the same way the earth wrinkled into the huge ridges we call mountains. At any rate, it became uncomfortable for the dinosaurs at about that time, when the Rockies and the Alps and the Andes were forming, and the big beasts did not survive to see the world in the shape we know it today.

The dinosaurs lived when the world was a fresh, juicy plum.

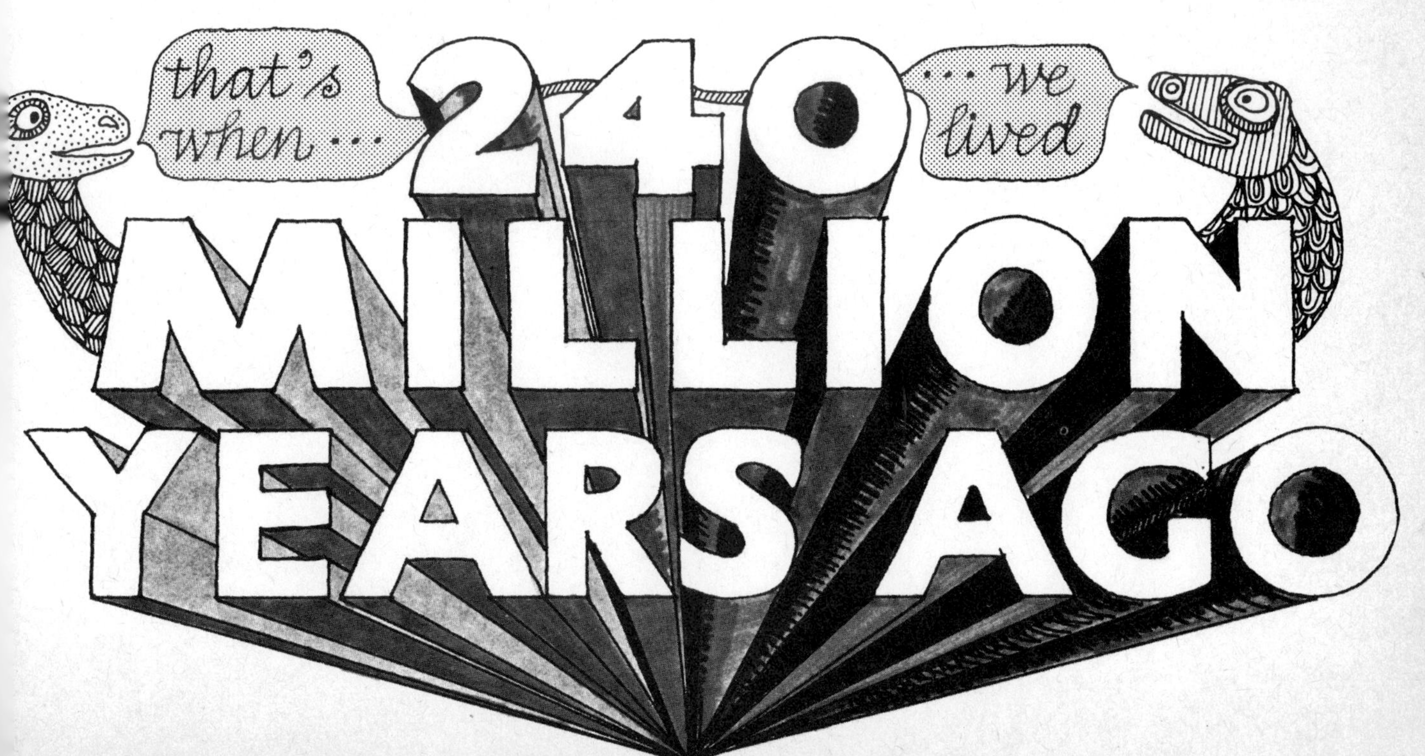

MAN IN THIS LITTLE SPACE AT THE TOP

If this page from bottom to top represents the time that has passed from the first dinosaurs until this moment, you can see that Man's entire existence takes up hardly more than the width of a pencil line.

DINOSAURS LIVING

NO DINOSAURS . . . .

But let's begin at the beginning – that's to say, in a haze of guesswork. We think that things first started moving about in the sea, which is a sensible guess, because there probably wasn't any land.

Since water has not changed since the beginning of the world, fish have hardly changed, either. They existed in much the same form five hundred million years ago and mostly remained the same ever since, unintellectual but efficient.

The lamprey – a surfeit of which killed King John – never even bothered to develop a jawbone. Possibly King John wished in his last moments that *he* hadn't either.

Some fish, though, *did* change. In the Devonian period – about three hundred and ninety-five million years ago – a few ambitious fish managed to develop rudimentary legs with fins on the end so that they could scramble out of the water.

The coelocanth, which still lives in the Indian Ocean, never got any further than these 'lobe fins' as they are called, and remains as a living link with prehistory.

Even more interesting is the lungfish, found nowadays in Africa, which digs a hole in the mud if the river dries up, and curls up safely inside this hole, *breathing air*. How about that for evolution?

Since the things that lived in the sea were so good at developing legs and lungs, it's not surprising that the first arrivals on land were amphibian creatures rather like newts. They were only suited to life in damp places, since they had to return to the water to lay their eggs, just as frogs do nowadays. One of the first of these amphibians was ichthyostega (say it 'ick-thee-o-stay-ga'), which looked rather like a crocodile but had five fingers on its hands and five toes on its feet.

At about this time, the plants went mad. They had been content to lead a seaweedy kind of life in the water, gradually putting out cautious fingers on to the land. Once they got the idea of roots, though, they started to run amok. The world was still warm and damp, and so huge tropical forests sprang up with trees thirty-five metres tall, even in places we think of as quite untropical, like Iceland and Birmingham. This period was called the Coal Age, because coal is made of the compressed remains of these rampant plants.

During the Coal Age, the first reptiles appeared. They were a distinct improvement on the amphibians because they laid their eggs on dry land as lizards do. This meant that they could venture further from the water and soon they were swarming everywhere. They learned to live in forests and deserts as well as in the swampy places where life had started. They found out how to run and jump and climb trees and some of them grew long ribs covered in skin which looked like wings, so that they could glide from tree to tree. These were called pterosaurs ('terro-saurs').

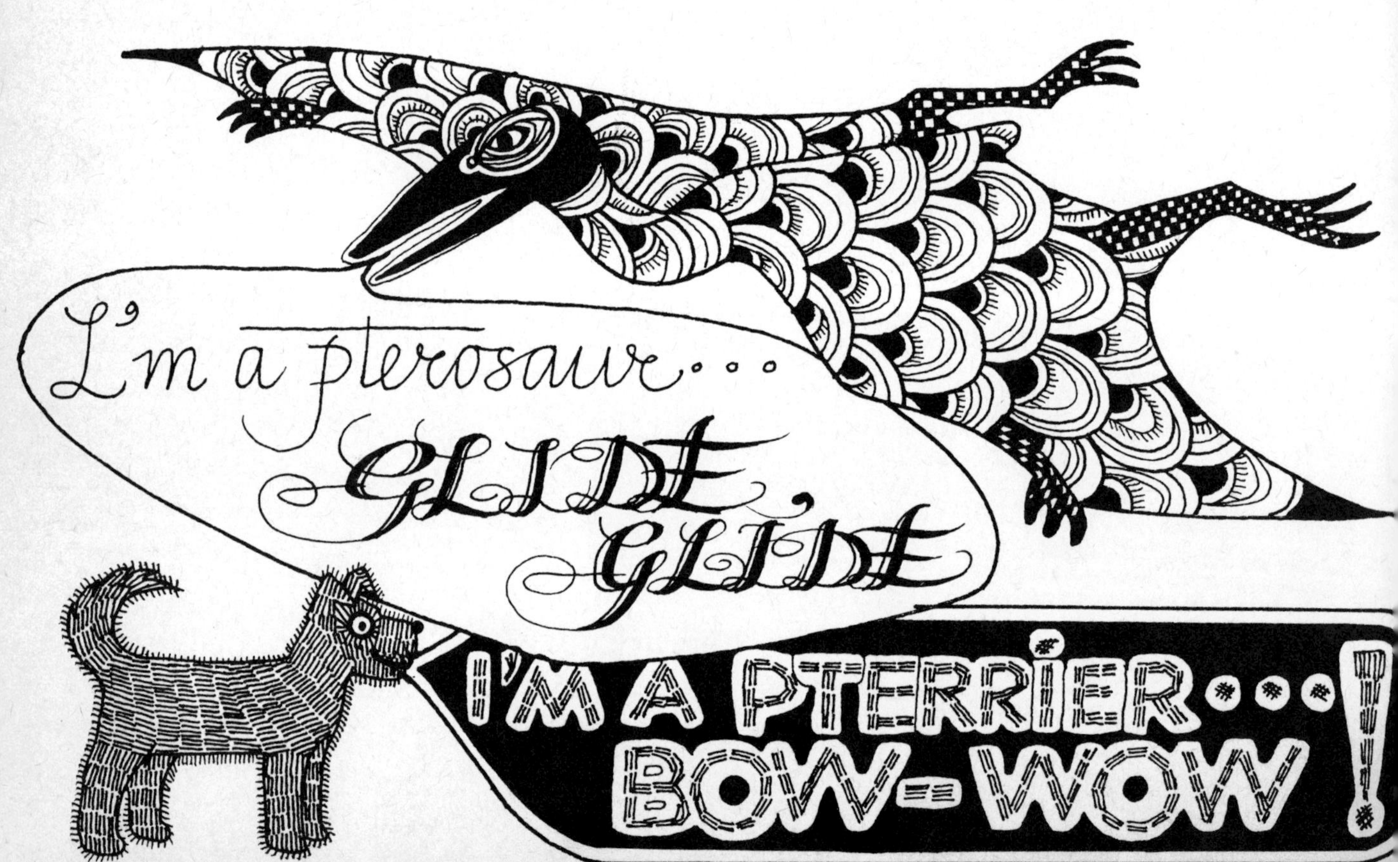

They must have enjoyed this gliding business because, as the centuries rolled past, they gradually adapted themselves even better to life in the air. The archaeopteryx ('arky-op-tericks') was an odd mixture between

lizard and bird, with a long, feather-covered lizard's tail and wings which had claws at the first joint. But the main bulk of these reptiles became what we know as dinosaurs.

Why do we call them dinosaurs? Quite simply, because the first dinosaur bones ever dug up scared everyone silly. Nobody had ever seen bones so large and so strange. Did they belong to a flying elephant, or a dragon, or what? After much prodding and debating, the professors decided that the bones must be those of a huge and ferocious lizard. So, being learned men who spoke Greek, they named the unknown beast with the Greek words for 'terrible lizard' – dinosaurus.

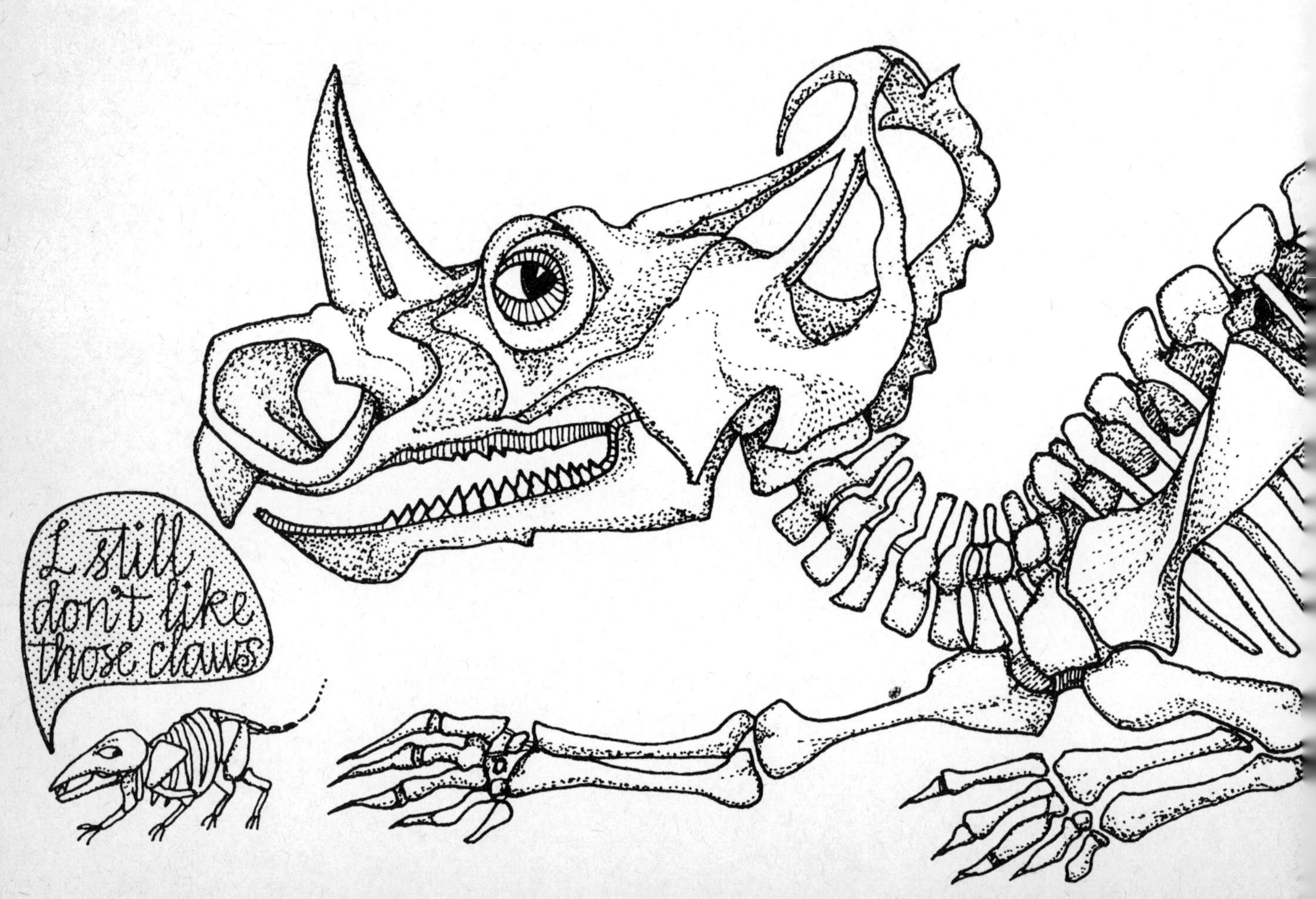

DINO
SAURUS
KNOCKING

After that the names came thick and fast as more and more bones were discovered. There was the little euparkeria (you-park-er-ear), for instance, which sounds like an Italian car-park.

The euparkeria was only the size of a goose, a funny little thing dashing about on its hind legs with its long tail stuck out behind it as a balancing pole to stop it falling flat on its face. It had short arms, was covered with scales, had a beak full of teeth, and was the early ancestor of the whole dinosaur family.

At this stage, early in the Triassic period, all the dinosaurs were small, some of them no bigger than chickens, and they all ran about on their hind legs. It was much later on, when they grew big and heavy, that they had to use their front legs to help support their weight.

After this the dinosaurs went on and on, and up and up.

They grew and spread, and developed lots of different families and generally set about ruling the roost for a hundred and thirty million years.

This enormous length of time divides itself roughly into three main periods. The first one was called the Triassic, and this was when the dinosaurs branched into two groups. According to the structure of their hip joints, these groups are called the 'lizard-hipped' and the 'bird-hipped'.

they call me lizard-hips. Are you a bird?
what do you think, darling?

Both the lizard-hipped and the bird-hipped dinosaurs were reptiles, and so they were cold-blooded. This might mean that they didn't think twice about killing things.

But it also means that they were warm and active when the sun shone, but cold and sluggish when it didn't.

This happened because the dinosaurs had no 'normal' temperature of their own but warmed up and cooled down according to the heat of their surroundings, as a stone would do. Humans, being warm-blooded, are not like stones.

Like all reptiles, dinosaurs laid leathery-shelled eggs which hatched into completely formed young dinosaurs, just as hens lay eggs which hatch into chickens.

Seven fossilised dinosaur eggs found in France in 1974 weighed six and a half pounds each, and were up to ten inches in diameter.

In the Triassic period most dinosaurs were placid vegetable-eaters – but there were one or two ferocious hunters which ate anything they could catch. The phytosaurus, for instance (say it 'fight-o-saurus'), looked very much like a crocodile and nobody was very sorry when he died out at the end of the Triassic period. Except, of course, the phytosaurus.

I'm not called phytosaurus for nothing. I'll phyt you to the death.
What's saurus for the goose is saurus for the gander. I'll phyt you, too.
Eek
Eek

Cynognathus ('sigh-nog-nay-thus') had a head rather like a bull-terrier, and so his name means 'dog-face'.

Dog-face himself was not a very polite beast. He killed and ate everything he could lay paws on. But he is very interesting for several reasons. He looked very much like a mammal – although he wasn't – and his legs were jointed with 'knees' and 'elbows' just as a modern animal's are. What's more, some scientists think he may even have had fur.

If that's his idea of a joke,
no wonder he died out.
Or did he?

Coelophysis ('seelo-fye-sis') was a pretty unscrupulous character, too. Although he was not very big (about the size of a horse) he would gobble up any living creature, including the young of his own species.

Aaargh! Dad! Put me down!
That's just what I'm going to do, son...
He always was Dad's favourite
I'm glad I wasn't!

But most of these early dinosaurs never dreamed of eating meat. Plateosaurus (rhyme it with 'matey-o-saurus')

and Yaleosaurus (yes, 'Yale-o-saurus') spent a peaceful life munching plants and wallowing gently in swampy places at the edge of the sun-warmed water.

The world must have been an amazingly lush place in those days, otherwise the plants and animals would never have grown to such an immense, overblown size. By the beginning of the Jurassic Period there were dinosaurs bigger than any land animal has been since.

A diplodocus found in America was three times as long as a London bus. Imagine *him* in Piccadilly in the rush hour!

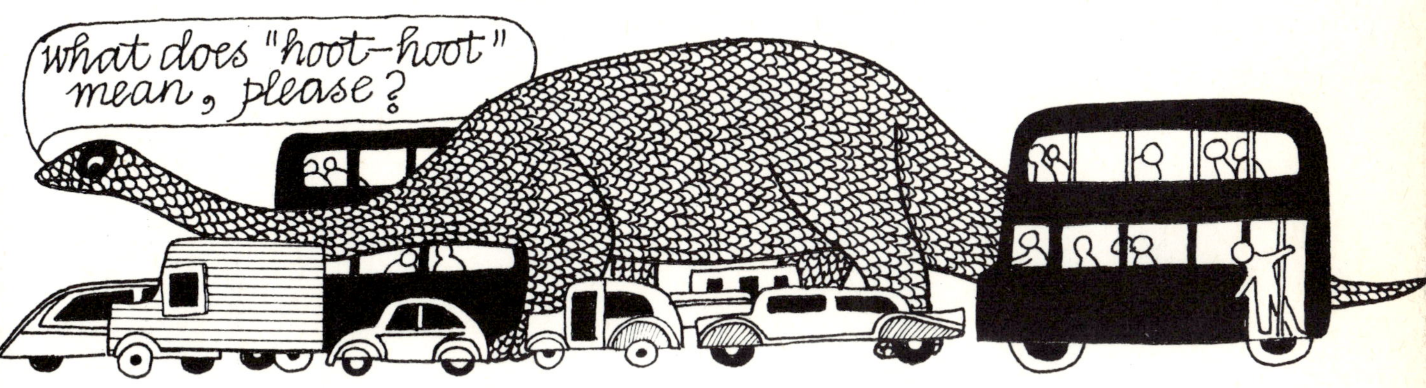

And brachiosaurus ('brakey-o-saurus') was seven times as heavy as an elephant.

Being so big and heavy, you would expect one of these huge beasts to make a deep hole each time he put his foot down, and to make a groove like a giant plough with the weight of his enormous tail. And as far as the footsteps go, you'd be right. Lots of fossilised footprints have been found in the kind of stone which, years ago, was mud, and the hole made by a hind foot held more water than you could put in your bath. But there were no tail marks. Could a dinosaur have held his hugely heavy tail in the air? Surely not!

It would have been very uncomfortable.

What he probably did was to paddle about in deep water like a fat uncle pretending he can swim, half-afloat but with his feet firmly on the bottom. That way, the dinosaur's tail floated on the surface of the water, like the uncle's legs.

Another thing which makes us think that most dinosaurs were mainly water animals is the fact that their eyes and nostrils were right on top of their heads, like a frog's are.

Brontosaurus (no, no, not Brontë-saurus!) and his cousins had blunt, rather ineffectual-looking teeth arranged in the front of his mouth like a garden rake. They were not strong enough to nibble at trees or graze on grass or even to rake gardens, but they must have been ideal for scooping up squishy mouthfuls of water weeds.

Had he survived, brontosaurus might have been the ideal cleaner-up of polluted lakes.

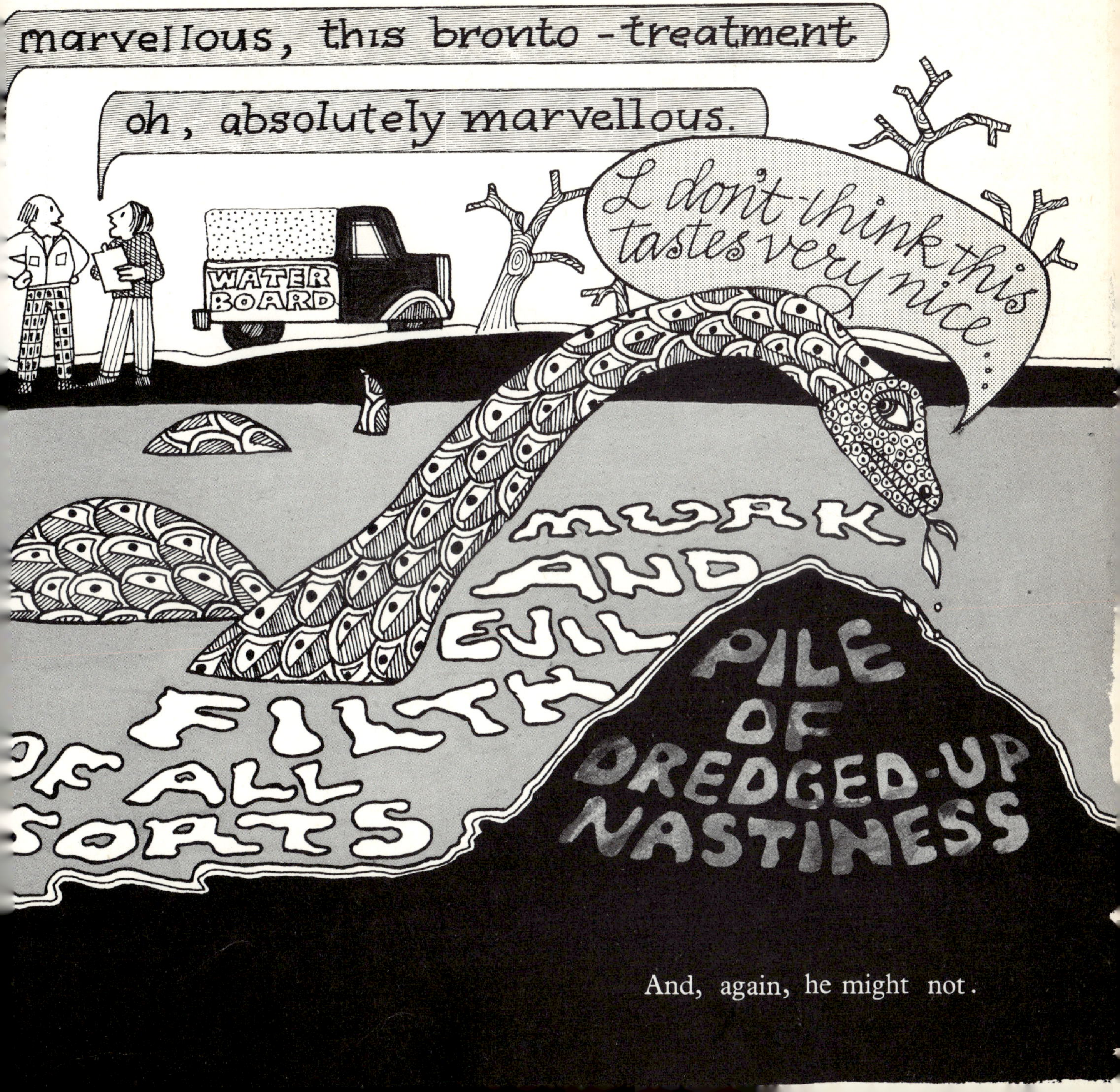

And, again, he might not.

The Cretaceous Period was a time of drastic changes. The earth had started to crumple up into mountain ranges and the general environment was probably changing rather faster than the dinosaurs could keep up with. To start with, the plants abandoned the idea of staying green all the year round and began to shed their leaves in the autumn.

This must have had a devastating effect on the dinosaurs. Many of them were very big indeed and they needed a lot of vegetable food each day to keep them going. What's more, the world no longer had an everlasting summer. There must have been some reason why the trees shed their leaves each year, and the simplest explanation is that it got cold. Winter, in fact, had arrived.

At the time things began to change in the Cretaceous Period, some of the dinosaurs began to develop weird, apparently meaningless variations. Pachycephalosaurus (packy-seff-allo-saurus') grew a layer of bone ten inches thick on the top of his head. That's as much as your head measures from ear to ear. Perhaps, since his brain was only the size of a walnut, he worried about protecting it. He certainly was the bone-head to end all bone-heads. But why did he need such a thick skull?

I can't doze a bull because they haven't been invented yet.

HE'S THICK

EEK!

perhaps he was an early kind of bulldozer?

TOC

TOC

TAC

Or perhaps he played tunes on his head with hammers?

It doesn't hurt any more, hooray!

Other dinosaurs, too, went in for heavy armour-plating. Ankylosaurus had rows of spikes all along his sides and must have found it quite hard to move about.

Styracosaurus grew elaborate horns all over his head,

and triceratops (say it 'try-serra-tops') had a built-in swords-and-shield arrangement with three spikes and a thick, bony frill round the back of his neck.

Then there was stegosaurus, whose name means 'plate lizard'. He looked like a walking artichoke, with pointed slabs of bone sticking up all along his back.

And then, of course, there was the king of them all, tyrannosaurus rex. Although he had silly little arms which couldn't reach his mouth, he stood as tall as six horses piled on top of each other. His head alone was the size of a Rolls Royce bonnet and he had ferocious saw-edged teeth curved like scimitars. He went roaring through what is now Northern Europe and America, terrorising everything that moved for a good few million years.

ARGH!
TA-RA!
WOOPS!
NEIGH
NAY
NO
ARE YOU ALL RIGHT?
SAG

But even tyrannosaurus had a thin time when the smaller dinosaurs faded away in the newly-cold winters. He was protected against all attack from larger animals but he never realised that he depended for his existence on the smaller ones.

What's more, like all dinosaurs, tyrannosaurus had a tiny little brain. Even in an animal the size of a Welsh chapel, the brain was hardly as big as a ping-pong ball. As a result, he not only lacked intellect, but also had a very poor control system. A dinosaur's left hand almost literally did not know what his right hand was doing.

In many ways, a dinosaur was rather like an old-fashioned signal box where levers were pulled to change the points. Just as the signal man thinks 'train coming – I must pull lever number six' so a dinosaur's brain would think 'right foot up' and set the muscles in motion to move his foot.

The trouble was that his brain was so underpowered that it sent out a very weak signal. To improve this, he had brain 'relays' further down his body. These were swollen sections of his spine which 'boosted' the signal so that it didn't fade away completely before it reached its destination. This way, he just about managed to keep all the parts of his huge body in touch with each other.

While the big dinosaurs were tramping about like the lords of the earth, other creatures were quietly evolving in their own way. The birds, for instance, tried a lot of variations. There was an odd creature called hesperornis, who looked like a seagull except that his beak was full of teeth and he had no wings at all.

Quite a lot of birds went in for legs rather than wings, and they grew to a huge size, much bigger than our present-day ostrich. The giant moas which used to live in New Zealand were nearly twice the size of a man.

While the dinosaurs were busy getting bigger and more complicated, some small, furry, shrew-like animals were scampering about in the undergrowth.

They were too small to be noticed by the big dinosaurs and too fast on their feet to be caught by the smaller ones. And, most important of all, they were mammals. Although the first mammals laid eggs and then fed the hatched-out babies with milk, they soon by-passed the egg-laying stage altogether and gave birth to living babies as we do. They were quick-thinking, warm-blooded and adaptable, and when the dinosaurs had disappeared into the darkness of the Great Unsolved Mystery the mammals lived on.

It's lucky for us that they came up with such a successful answer to the survival problem. Otherwise at this very moment we might all be something else instead of people.

And would that have been such a bad thing?
Nobody knows.
Not even the dinosaurs.

INDEX